WIPE-CLEAN LEARNING

T0044675

Early
MATH

AUTUMN PUBLISHING

Counting 1–10

Complete the dot-to-dots.

1 3 5 7 9
2 4 6 8 10

1 2 3 4 5 6 7 8 9 10

1 2 3 4 5 6 7 8 9 10

Now try tracing these:

1 2 3 4 5

Trace the numbers.

6 7 8 9 10

Counting 1–20

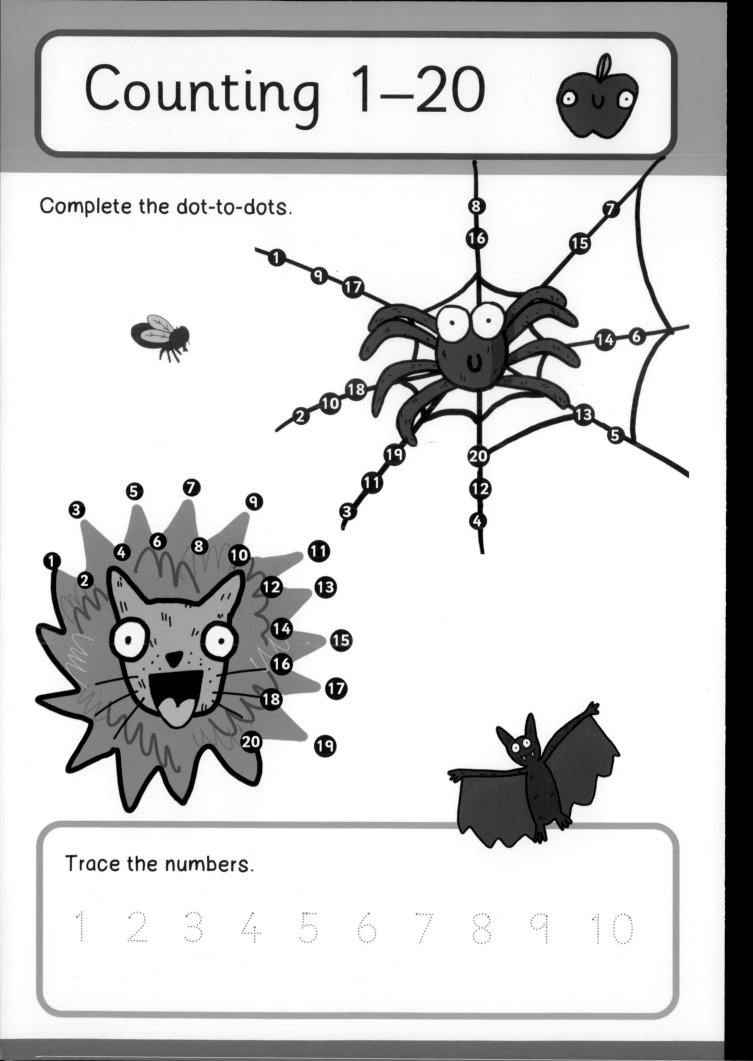

Complete the dot-to-dots.

Trace the numbers.

1 2 3 4 5 6 7 8 9 10

Trace the numbers.

11 12 13 14 15 16 17 18 19 20

Adding

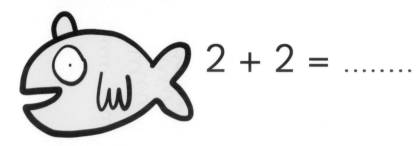

Add two more fins to the fish.
How many fins does it have now?

$2 + 2 =$ ....

Add six legs to the octopus.
How many legs does it have now?

$2 + 6 =$ ....

Add four more teeth to
the shark. How many
teeth does it have now?

$2 + 4 =$ ....

Trace the sums.

$1 + 1 = 2$ $1 + 2 = 3$

Add two more windows to the rocket.
How many does it have now?

$1 + 2 = $ ....

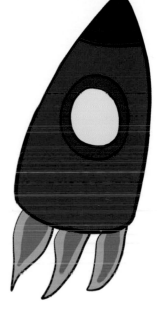

Draw four more stars.
How many are there
in total?

$2 + 4 = $ ....

Draw three more eyes on the alien.
How many are there now?

$1 + 3 = $ ....

Trace the sums.

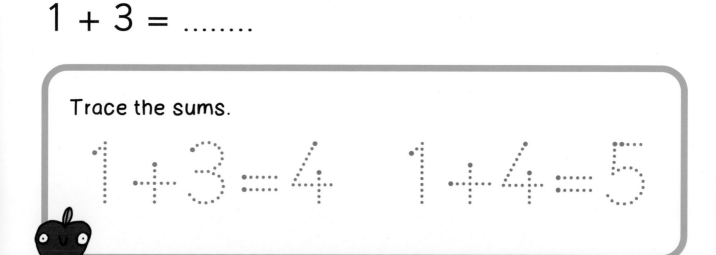

$1 + 3 = 4$ $1 + 4 = 5$

More adding

Draw nine buttons on the calculator.

Draw two more straps on the school bag. How many are there now?

2 + 2 = ...

Draw two crayons for the koala, then draw one more. How many are there in total?

2 + 1 = ...

Trace the sums.

1 + 5 = 6   1 + 6 = 7

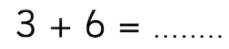

Add six wheels under the train cars. How many wheels are there in total?

3 + 6 = ...

Add four more windows to the bus.

Add one funnel.

Trace the sums.

1 + 7 = 8   1 + 8 = 9

Doubling

Draw two more bees.

How many are there now? ☐

Trace the sums.

$1 + 1 = 2$ $2 + 2 = 4$

Draw four more books.

How many are there now?

Trace the sums.

$3+3=6$ $4+4=8$

More doubling

Draw five more thumbtacks.

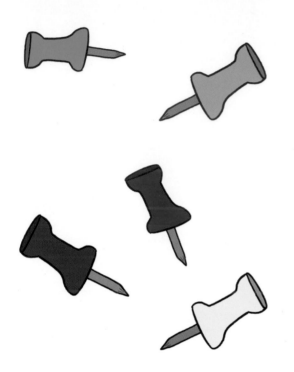

How many are there now? ☐

Trace the sums.

$$5 + 5 = 10 \qquad 6 + 6 = 12$$

Draw seven more butterflies.

How many are there now?

Trace the sums.

7+7=14 8+8=16

Halving

Cross out half of these trophies.

How many are left? ☐

Trace the calculations.

2 — 1 = 1   4 — 2 = 2

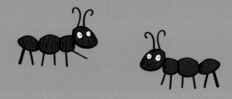

Cross out half of these weights.

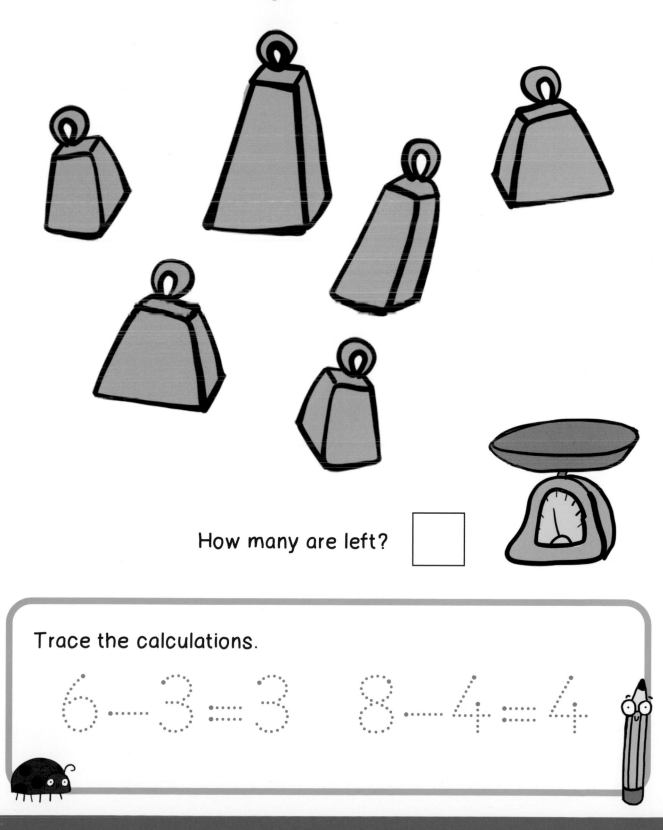

How many are left?

Trace the calculations.

6 − 3 = 3   8 − 4 = 4

More halving

Cross out half of these socks.

How many are left? ☐

Trace the calculations.

10–5=5   12–6=6

Cross out half of these racing cars.

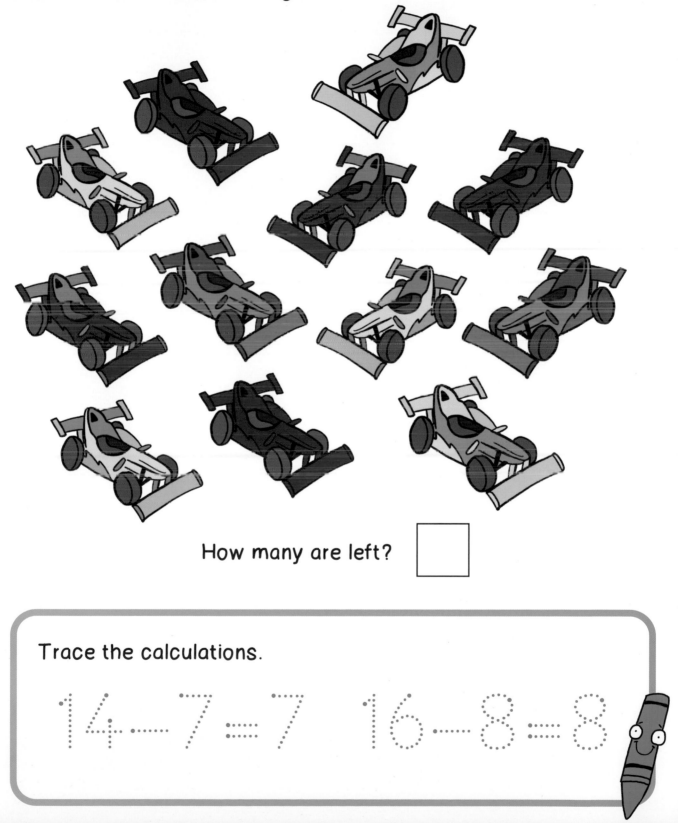

How many are left? ☐

Trace the calculations.

14 − 7 = 7   16 − 8 = 8

Draw a line through the middle of each shape to halve it.

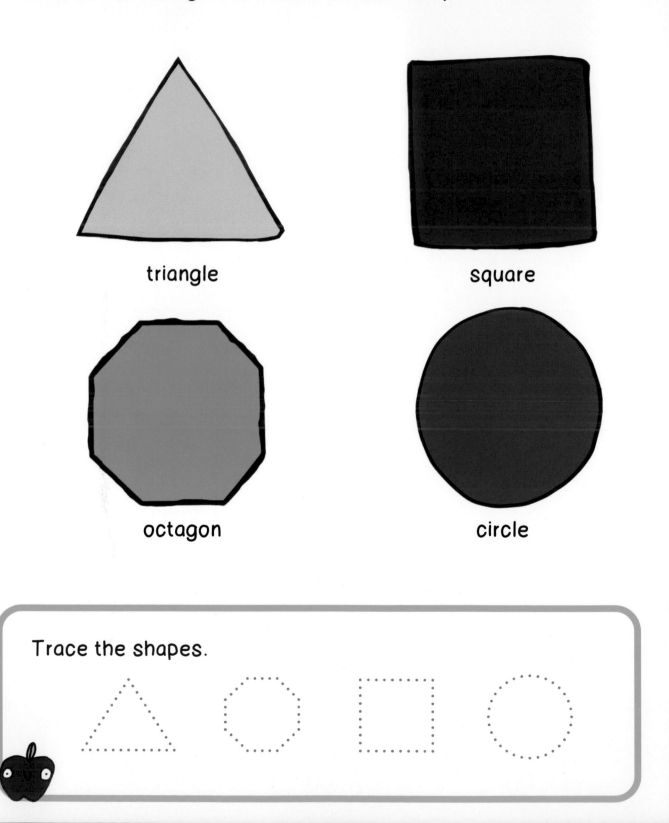

triangle

square

octagon

circle

Trace the shapes.

Draw two lines through each shape to split it into quarters.

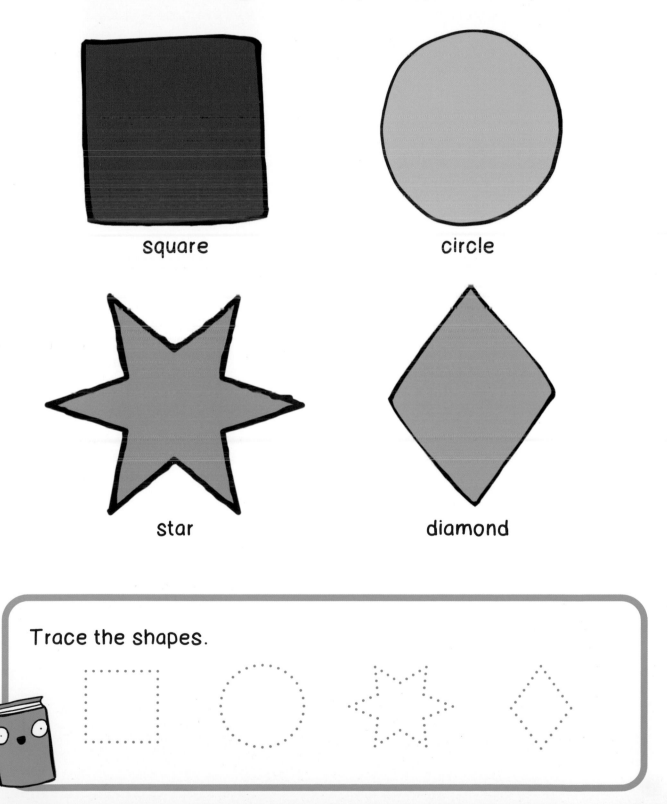

square

circle

star

diamond

Trace the shapes.

Grouping

Draw a circle around ten penguins.

How many penguins are not circled?

Keep circling groups of five bananas until you have fewer than five left.

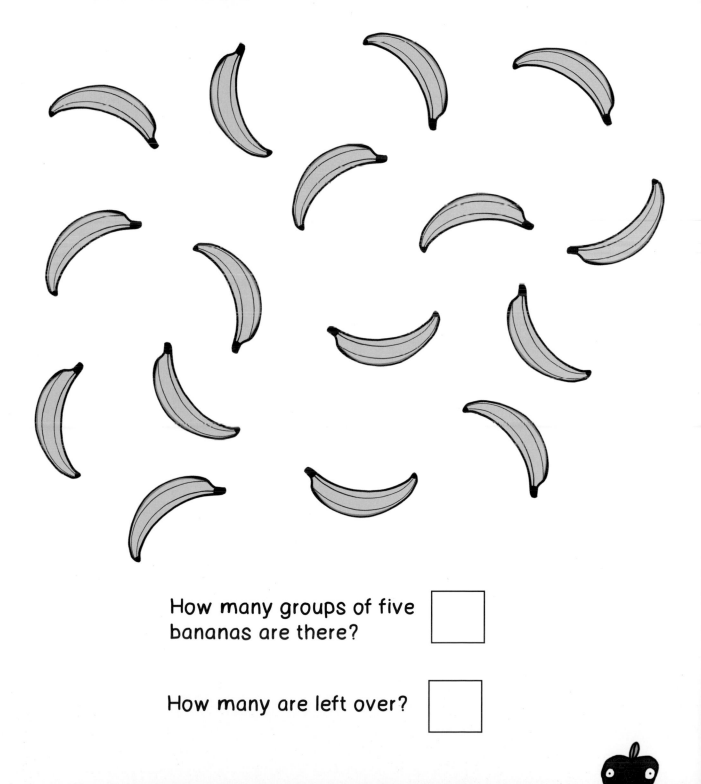

How many groups of five bananas are there? ☐

How many are left over? ☐

Odd and even

This frog only jumps on even-numbered lily pads. Can you draw a jumping line from each even lily pad to the next?

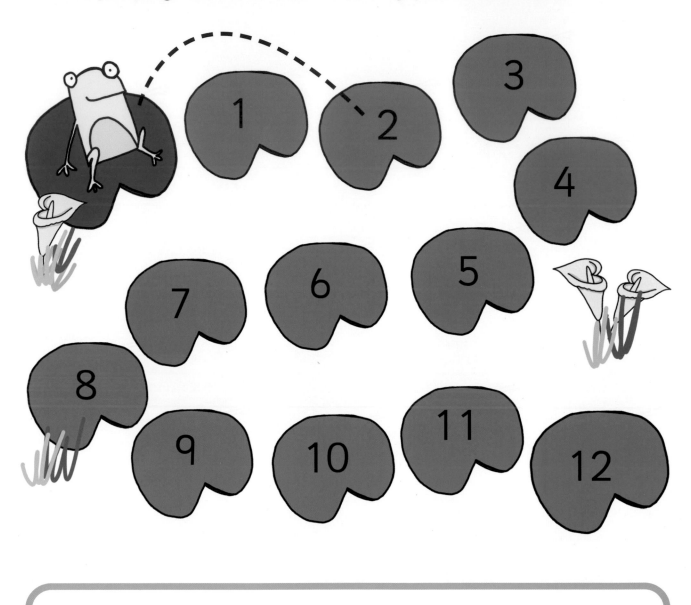

Trace the sequence.

2 4 6 8 10 12

This frog only jumps on odd-numbered lily pads. Can you draw a jumping line from each odd lily pad to the next?

Trace the sequence.

1 3 5 7 9 11

Sequences

Fill in the missing numbers in each sequence.

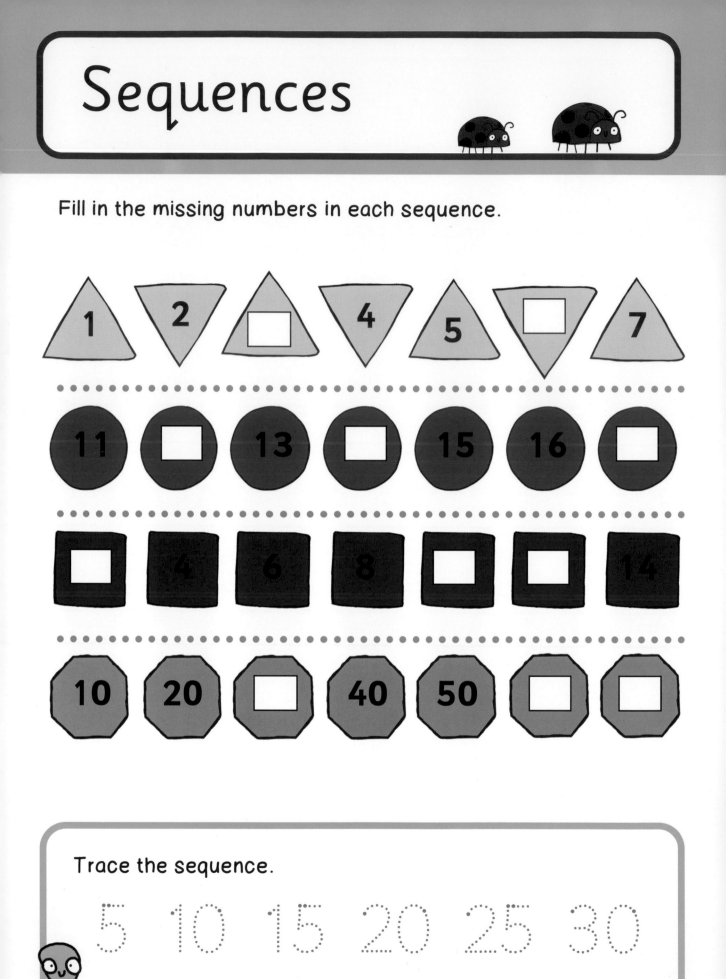

1 2 ☐ 4 5 ☐ 7

11 ☐ 13 ☐ 15 16 ☐

☐ 4 6 8 ☐ ☐ 14

10 20 ☐ 40 50 ☐ ☐

Trace the sequence.

5 10 15 20 25 30

Numbers

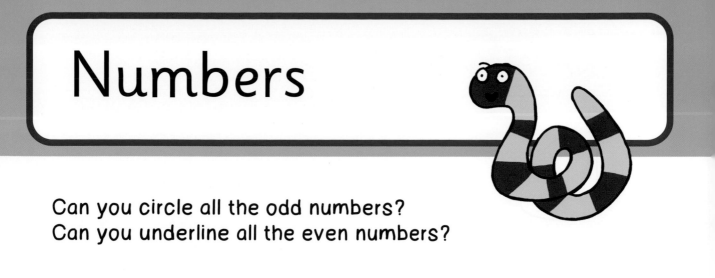

Can you circle all the odd numbers?
Can you underline all the even numbers?

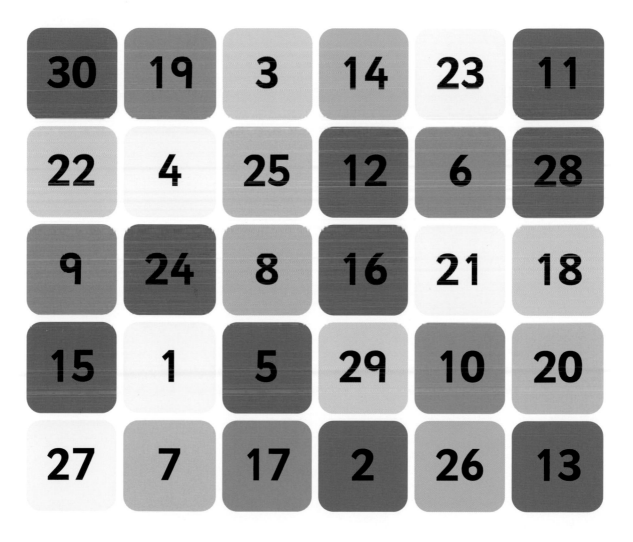

30	19	3	14	23	11
22	4	25	12	6	28
9	24	8	16	21	18
15	1	5	29	10	20
27	7	17	2	26	13

Shape sequences

Draw the correct shapes in the blank spaces.

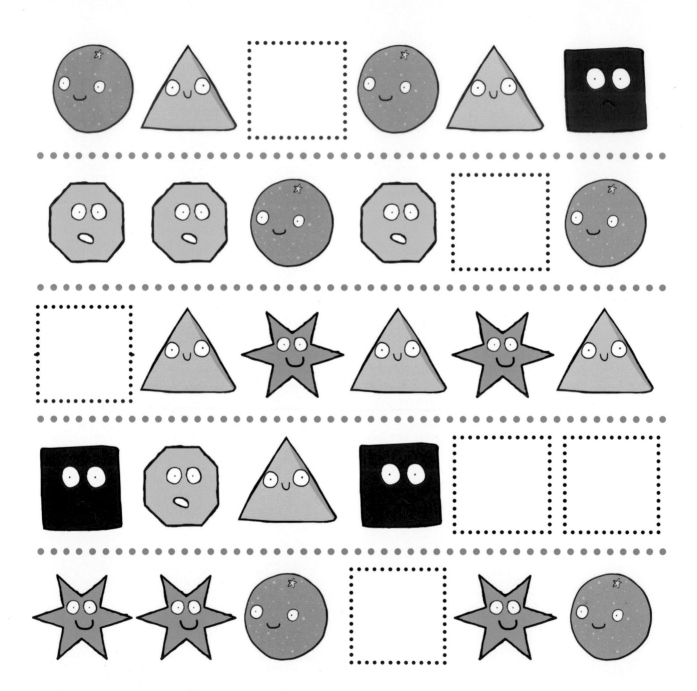

In this sudoku, there can only be one of each shape in a row and column. Which shape is missing from the grid? Draw it in the space.

Number bonds to 10

Write the correct numbers in the empty boxes.

9 + □ = **10**

□ + 6 = **10**

□ + 8 = **10**

Trace the numbers.

1   2   3   4   5

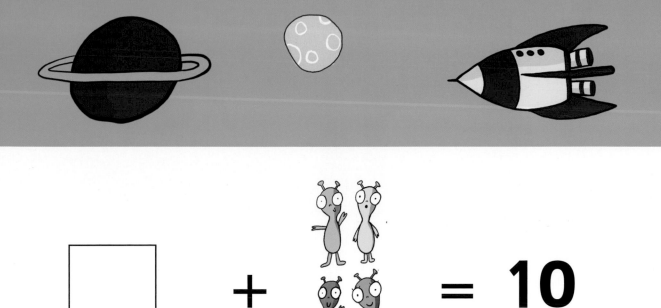

☐ + 🛸🛸🛸🛸 = **10**

🛸🛸 + ☐ = **10**

☐ + 🛸🛸🛸🛸🛸 = **10**

Trace the numbers.

6 7 8 9 10

Write the correct numbers in the empty boxes.

$$+ \boxed{} = \textbf{20}$$

$$+ \boxed{} = \textbf{20}$$

$$\boxed{} + \quad = \textbf{20}$$

Trace the numbers.

1 2 3 4 5 6 7 8 9 10

□ + 🍉🍉🍉🍉🍉🍉🍉🍉🍉🍉 = **20**

⭐⭐⭐⭐ + □ = **20**

🍾🍾🍾🍾🍾🍾 + □ = **20**

Trace the numbers.

11 12 13 14 15 16 17 18 19 20

Counting on

Count on 3 more from 1.

1 2 3 4 5 6 7 8 9 10

Count on 4 more from 5.

1 2 3 4 5 6 7 8 9 10

Count on 5 more from 3.

1 2 3 4 5 6 7 8 9 10

Count on 6 more from 4.

1 2 3 4 5 6 7 8 9 10

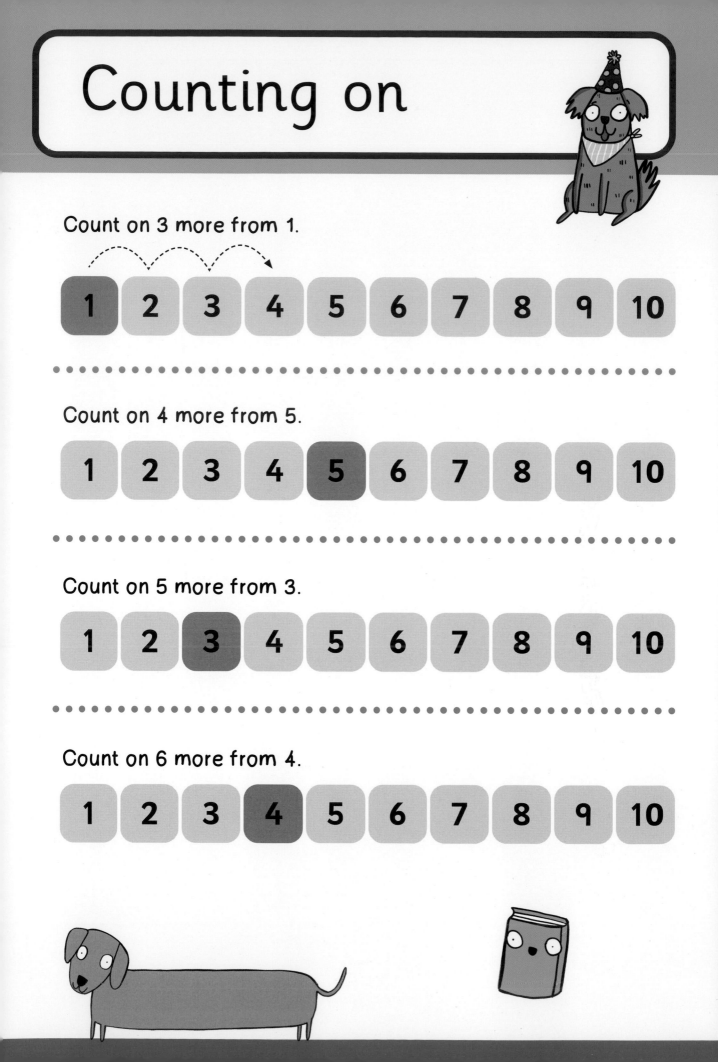

Count on 2 more from 17.

| 11 | 12 | 13 | 14 | 15 | 16 | **17** | 18 | 19 | 20 |

Count on 5 more from 13.

| 11 | 12 | **13** | 14 | 15 | 16 | 17 | 18 | 19 | 20 |

Count on 6 more from 11.

| **11** | 12 | 13 | 14 | 15 | 16 | 17 | 18 | 19 | 20 |

Count on 3 more from 15.

| 11 | 12 | 13 | 14 | **15** | 16 | 17 | 18 | 19 | 20 |

More adding

Can you add these objects?

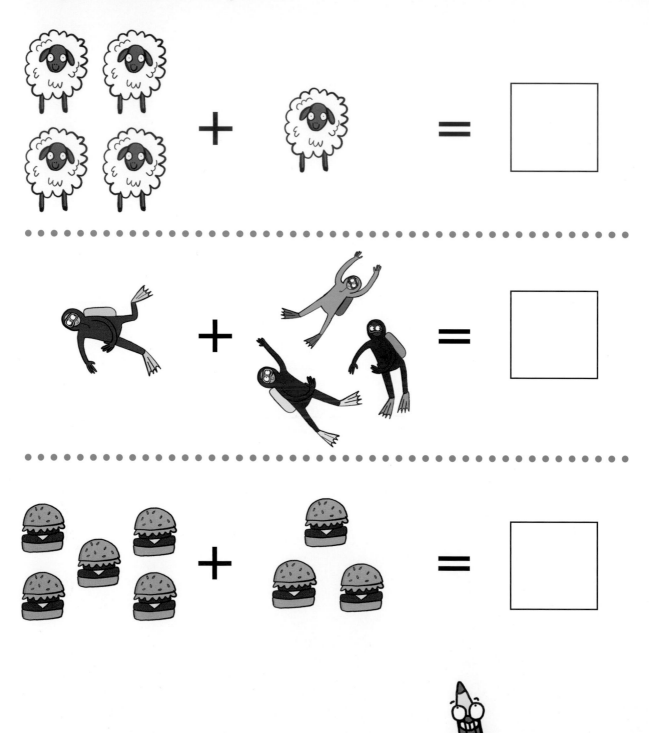

Can you add these objects?

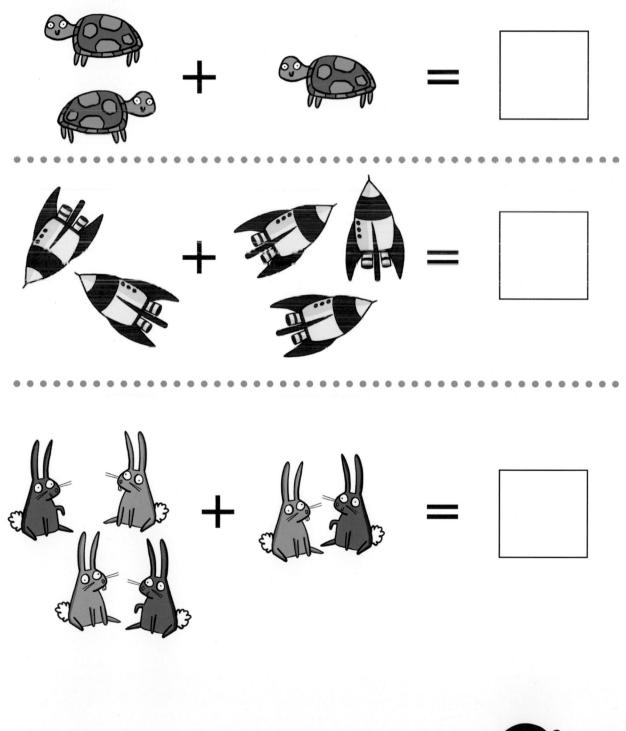

Subtracting

Can you subtract these objects?

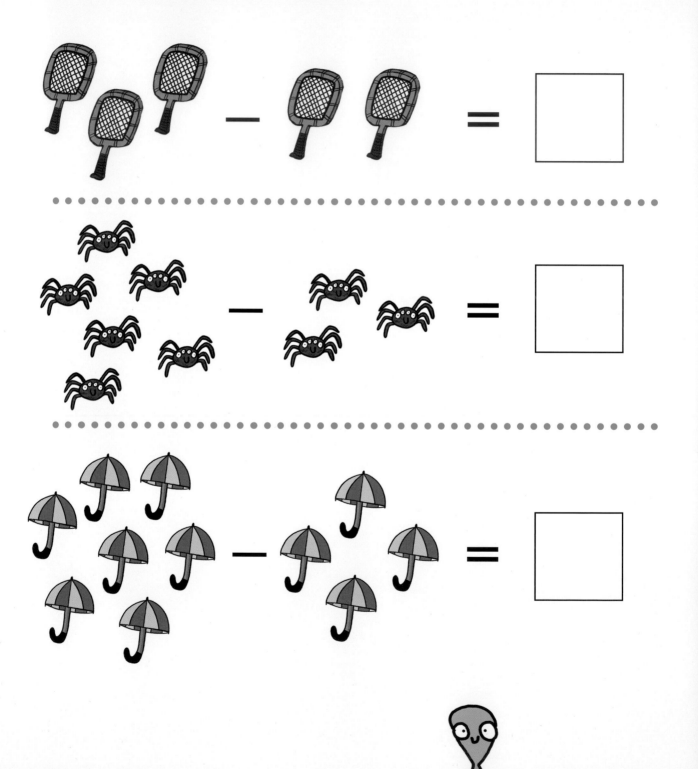

Multiply by 2

Use the objects to help you complete the calculations.

2 × 2 = ☐

2 × 3 = ☐

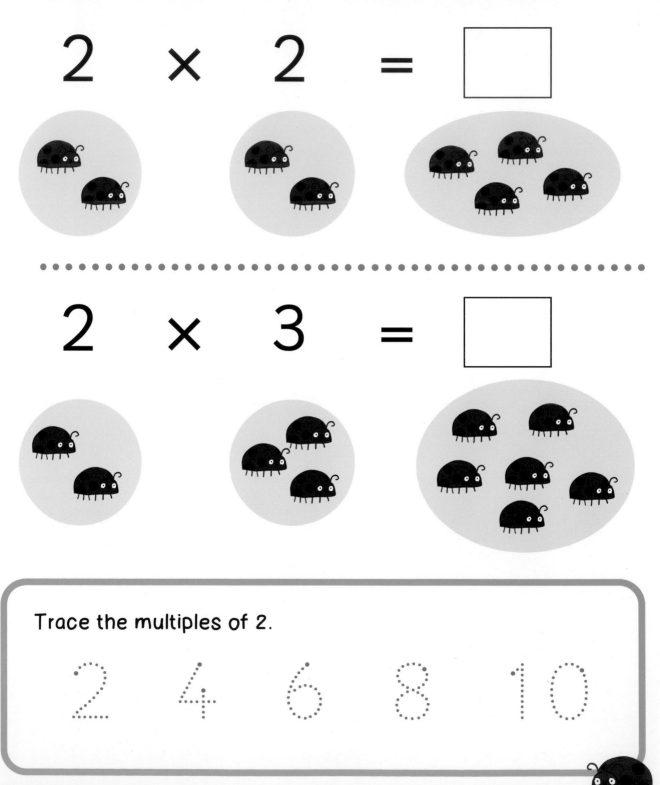

Trace the multiples of 2.

2 4 6 8 10

Use the objects below to work out how to multiply.

2 × 4 = ▢

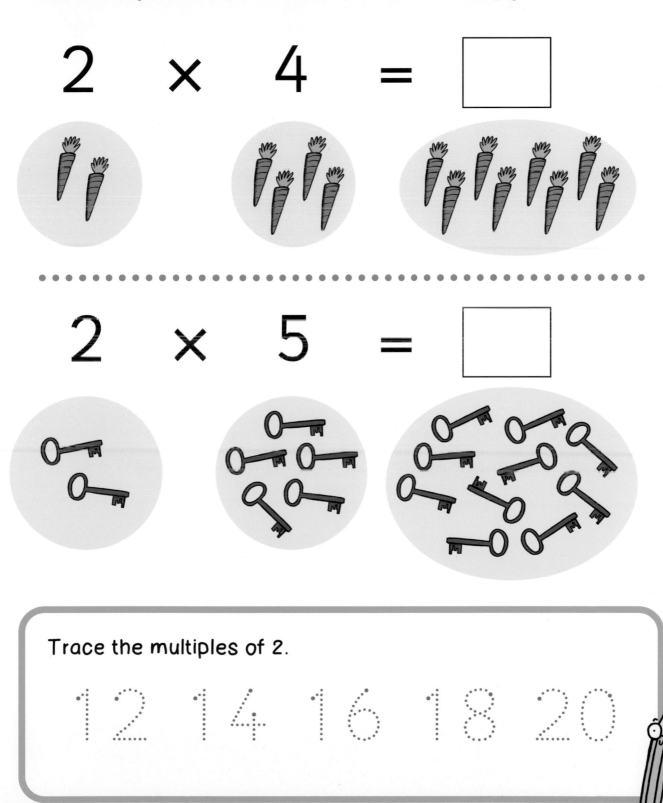

2 × 5 = ▢

Trace the multiples of 2.

12 14 16 18 20

Multiply by 5

Use the objects to help you complete the calculations.

$$5 \times 2 = \boxed{}$$

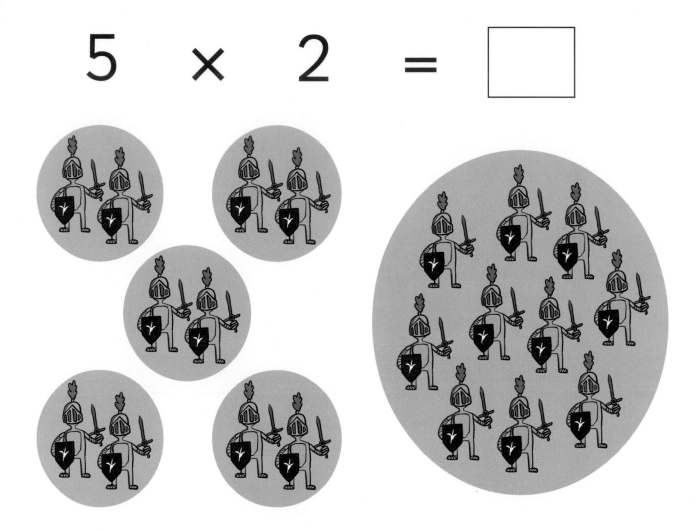

Trace the multiples of 5.

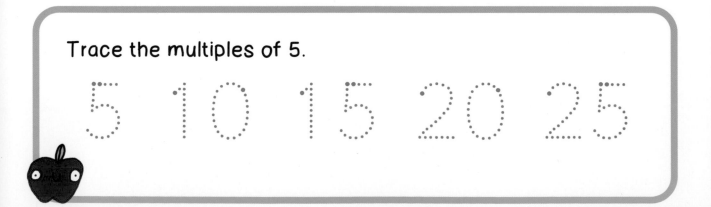

5 10 15 20 25

Draw three coins in each of the small circles, then draw the total number of coins in the large circle. Count the total to answer the calculation.

5 × 3 =

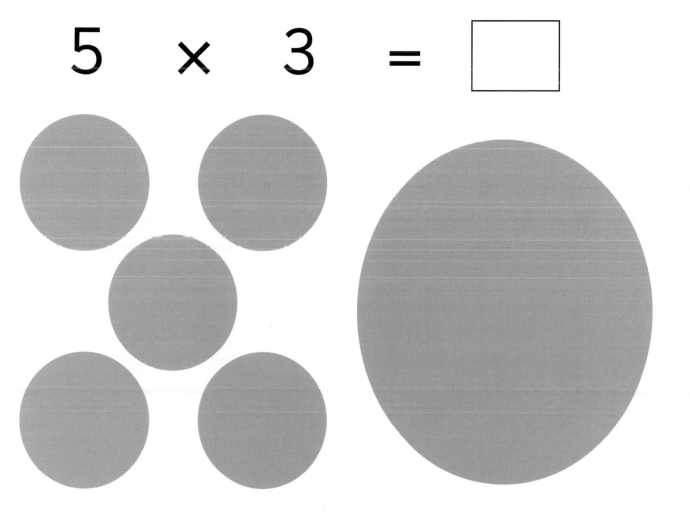

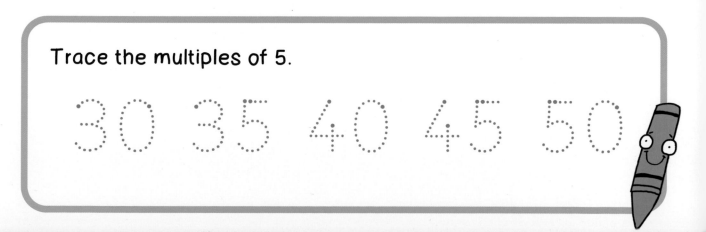

Trace the multiples of 5.

30 35 40 45 50

Multiply by 10

Use the objects below to work out how to multiply.

10 × 2 = ☐

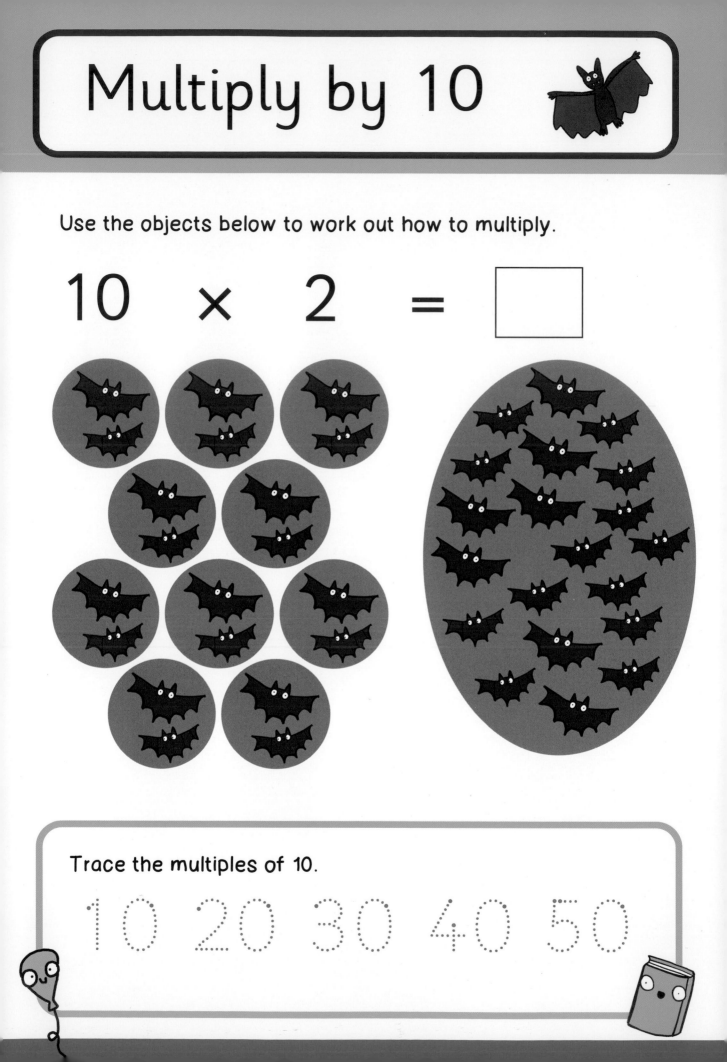

Trace the multiples of 10.

10 20 30 40 50

Draw three coins in each of the small circles, then draw the total number of coins in the large circle. Count the total to answer the calculation.

10 × 3 = ☐

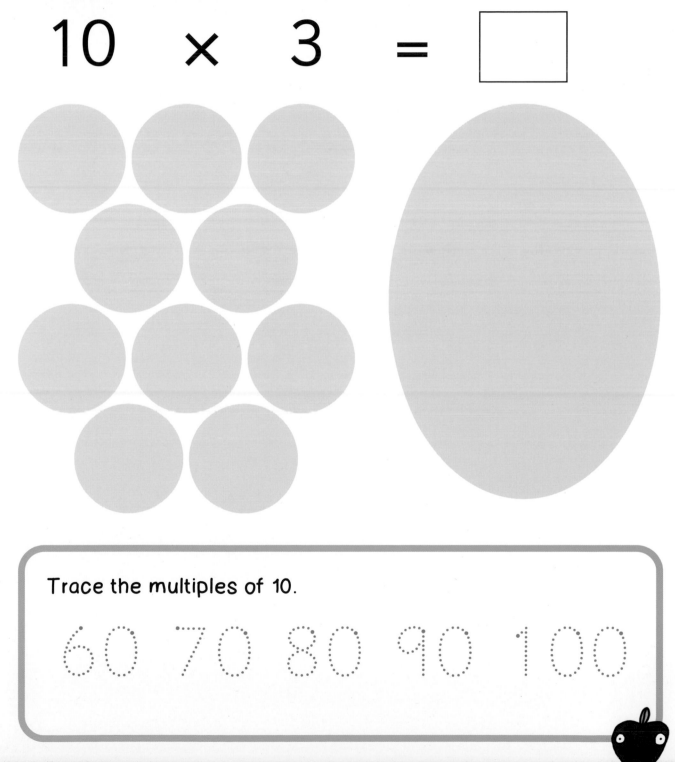

Trace the multiples of 10.

60 70 80 90 100

Simple sums

Trace the calculations, then write the answers.

1 + 1 = ☐

2 + 2 = ☐

3 + 3 = ☐

4 + 4 = ☐

5 + 5 = ☐

6 + 6 = ☐

7 + 7 = ☐

8 + 8 = ☐

9 + 9 = ☐

10 + 10 = ☐

Trace the number bonds to 10, then write the answers.
Some have missing numbers—can you fill them in?

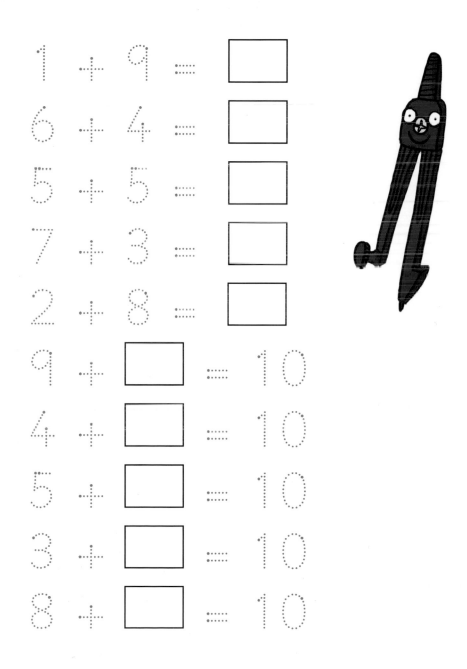

1 + 9 = ☐

6 + 4 = ☐

5 + 5 = ☐

7 + 3 = ☐

2 + 8 = ☐

9 + ☐ = 10

4 + ☐ = 10

5 + ☐ = 10

3 + ☐ = 10

8 + ☐ = 10

WIPE-CLEAN LEARNING

Give your child a head start at school with this big book of games and activities, reviewed by educational experts. Then wipe the pages clean and play all over again!

AUTUMN PUBLISHING

autumnpublishing.co.uk

First published in the UK by Autumn Publishing
An imprint of Igloo Books Ltd
Cottage Farm, NN6 0BJ, UK
Owned by Bonnier Books
Sveavägen 56, Stockholm, Sweden
All rights reserved, including the right of
reproduction in whole or in part in any form.
Educational consultant: Carrie Lewis
Illustrated by Katie Abey
Designed by Lee Italiano
Edited by Rebecca Kealy
Manufactured in China. 0423 001
10 9 8 7 6 5 4 3 2 1

US $8.99
CAN $11.99

Climate Neutral Product

3+

Conforms to ASTM D4236

⚠ **WARNING:**
CHOKING HAZARD – Small parts.
Not for children under 3 yrs.

ISBN 978-1-83852-788-4

50899

9 781838 527884